LEEDS TRINITY UNIVERSITY

Published by Grafton Books 1986

Grafton Books
A Division of the Collins Publishing Group
8 Grafton Street, London W1X 3LA

Designed and produced by Templar Publishing Company Ltd,
Old King's Head Court, Dorking, Surrey

Text copyright © Darrell Waters Limited 1949
This edition and illustrations copyright © Templar Publishing Limited 1986

First published by Macmillan & Co Ltd, London 1949

Blyton, Enid
The Last Supper; & other stories. – (Enid Blyton's Bible stories; 11)
1. Bible stories, English – N.T.
I. Title II. Horne, Penny III. Series 225.9'505   BS2401

ISBN 0-246-13105-5 (cased)
ISBN 0-583-31074-5 (limp)

Printed in Spain by Cayfosa. Barcelona
Dep. Leg. B-23834-1986

Enid Blyton's
·BIBLE·STORIES·

THE
LAST SUPPER

NEW TESTAMENT

GRAFTON BOOKS
A Division of the Collins Publishing Group

LONDON GLASGOW
TORONTO SYDNEY AUCKLAND

THE LAST SUPPER

J udas was one of the disciples of Jesus. He was clever, and the others trusted him to do many things for them.

"You can go and bargain in the town for the food we need," they said to Judas. "We have very little money and you can make the best of what we have. You are good at dealing with money and keeping account of it."

Judas was a strange man. Although he was one of the disciples, he did not love Jesus. The only person he really loved was himself.

At first he had believed in Jesus, and thought He was a very wonderful man, so powerful that it would not be long before He became a king.

"And when He is King, He will remember all His disciples and friends," thought the cunning Judas, "and I shall be among them. I shall become a prince, at least! I shall have much power and a great deal of money.''

The months went by and Judas found that Jesus was certainly not going to be the kind of king that Judas imagined. And what was this kingdom that Jesus so often spoke of? Why, it was only a kingdom of love! It wasn't a real kingdom with palaces and soldiers and courtiers and plenty of money flowing in—it was simply a kingdom of love, to which the poorest of the land could belong.

Judas was scornful of such a kingdom. He had not given up his work to follow Jesus for that!

''This man is full of a strange power. He can work the most wonderful miracles,'' thought Judas. ''Then why does He not work miracles for Himself and for us? He could so easily make us rich and strong and powerful! But He doesn't. He simply goes round talking and preaching, and

healing the sick. I wish I had never followed Him!"

The traitor said nothing to the others of what he thought. Then one day he became afraid. Some of the powerful men of Jerusalem, the Chief Priests, the Scribes and the Pharisees, were making threats against Jesus. They were angry because the poor people loved Him, followed Him and believed every word He said. They were jealous and bitter.

Judas knew this. He knew that if the Chief Priests could take Jesus and throw Him into prison with His disciples, they would be glad.

"I don't want to go to prison," thought Judas. "I must look after myself. I will go to the Chief Priests and tell them I will help them to capture Jesus, if they will pay me. Then I shall be safe."

Now it happened that Caiaphas, the High Priest, was calling a meeting of the rulers of Jerusalem to decide how they could take Jesus and put Him into prison.

"We will capture Him as soon as we can," said Caiaphas. "But not just yet. There is a great Festival in Jerusalem this week, and the town is full of people who love Jesus. We will wait till the week is over, then we will see what we can do to take this man."

Someone came into the room where they were holding their meeting, someone who made the priests stare in amazement.

It was Judas—Judas, one of the very disciples of the man they had been talking of. What did he want?

He soon told them. "I will help you to capture Jesus," said Judas. "How much will you give me if I do?"

This made things very easy for the priests. They were delighted. "We will give you thirty pieces of silver!" said Caiaphas. "That is the price of a slave, and is good pay for you."

"Pay me now," said Judas. he didn't trust anyone because he was untrustworthy himself. The priests counted out thirty pieces of silver for the traitor.

"I will send you word when you can capture Jesus," said Judas. "I will choose a time when there are few people about to interfere."

Then he left the meeting with the money in his

bag—and with a terrible secret in his heart.
"Nobody guesses what I have done," he thought.
"I have sold Jesus for thirty peices of silver. I am
rich!"

But Jesus knew what he had done, and He was grieved and sad at heart.

It was Festival Week in Jerusalem. The sacred Feast of the Passover was being held. Jesus

wanted to eat the Feast for the last time with His disciples, before He was betrayed by Judas.

"Go and prepare the Feast in a room I will tell you of," said Jesus to Peter and John. So the two disciples went to the room that a friend had lent to Jesus for the feast, and got it ready.

Round the table were drawn couches, for in those long-ago days people lay on couches to eat their meals and did not sit on chairs. The feast was of bread made without yeast, roast lamb, a sauce, a bitter salad, and wine to drink. Peter and John prepared everything ready for the meal.

Some of the disciples wanted to take the chief seats at the table. Jesus saw this. Had they still not learnt that such things did not matter? How could he show them that it was wrong and foolish always to try and get the best seats, the finest food, the most attention?

Now usually at a feast there was a servant who

welcomed the guests, and brought water to wash their dirty, dusty feet. But there was no servant that night.

"I will be their servant," thought Jesus. "I will show them that although I am called Master by them all, I am their humble and loving servant too, as we all should be to one another."

He took off his long cloak and wide belt, and tied a towel round His waist. He took water and poured it into a basin on the floor. And then Jesus went from one disciple to another, washing and wiping their feet.

The disciples were astonished. Peter tried to stop Jesus from washing his feet—but when Jesus said, "He that would be chief among you shall be servant of all," he and the others knew what Jesus meant, and they were silent.

The great Feast began. Jesus broke the bread and blessed it, and then gave it to His disciples.

He handed them the cup of wine, bidding each
one drink of it.

He told them that the broken bread and the
red wine were like His body, which would be

broken, and like His blood, which would be spilt.

"This is my body, and this is my blood," He said.

Then He told the disciples that He was soon to die, but that He would come again to them before He went up to His Father in Heaven.

And still we keep this Feast ourselves and call it the Holy Communion, eating bread, drinking wine, and remembering how Jesus gave His body and His blood for all of us who welcome His kingdom of love. It is our Feast of Remembrance, our way of coming close to the Lord and Master.

When Jesus and His disciples had finished their supper—the last one that Jesus had with them—Judas slipped away.

The time had come for him to betray Jesus. It was dark. Judas knew that soon Jesus was going into the lonely Garden of Gethsemane with His disciples. It would be a good time for the priests to send and take him.

Jesus waited until Judas had gone. Then He gave His disciples a new commandment—the very greatest and most important of all His commandments.

"I give you a new commandment," He said.

"Love one another."

He did not give it only to His disciples. He gave it to us as well. It is a commandment we should never forget.

Then Jesus arose and took His disciples to the quiet Garden of Gethsemane. He left all but Peter, James and John at the gate. He wanted these three near Him, because He was very sad.

He knew that His work on earth was finished, and that soon some very terrible things would happen to Him. Judas had gone to betray Him. Jesus needed to pray and to get courage and comfort from His Heavenly Father. Although He was the Son of God He was also the Son of Man, and He felt the same things that we feel, and suffered pain and unhappiness just as we do.

"Wait here and keep awake," He said to the three disciples, and He went a little way away to pray.

After a while He went back to His disciples, feeling lonely and unhappy. They were all asleep.

"Could you not keep awake for me one hour?" said Jesus, sadly, and once again He went to pray to God. He knew that in a very short time Judas would come with soldiers to take Him.

Jesus went to His disciples twice more—and at the third time His face was full of courage.

"Rise!" He said. "Let us be gone. Our betrayer is here."

Judas had been to Caiaphas. "Go now to the Garden of Gethsemane," he said. "Jesus is there with His disciples. It will be easy to take Him there, in the dark of night."

There came a noise at the gate, and in marched soldiers, priests, servants and the Temple Guard. They were armed with sticks and swords. They carried torches, and the flames lighted up the olive trees in the Garden.

"Judas, how shall we know which man is Jesus?" asked the priests.

"I will go to Him and kiss Him," said Judas. "You must watch to see which man I greet, and take Him."

Judas went straight up to Jesus, who was

standing silently beneath an olive tree.

"Hail, Master!" said Judas, and kissed Him, as was his custom.

Jesus looked at him sadly and sternly. "Judas, do you betray me with a kiss?" He said. Then He turned to the crowd of excited men nearby.

"Whom do you seek?" He asked.

"Jesus of Nazareth," they answered.

"I am He," said Jesus.

Peter drew his sword, ready to defend Jesus to the death. He struck out at a man nearby.

"Peter, put away your sword," commanded Jesus. He turned to the crowd once more.

"Have you come against me as if I were a thief, with sticks and swords? You laid no hand on me when I sat each day in the Temple, preaching. But now your time has come—this is your hour, and the powers of evil must have their way."

Then the soldiers laid hands on Jesus and took Him. And all His disciples forsook Him and fled.

Peter followed the soldiers and priests a good way behind. He was afraid. How terrible to see Jesus, so wonderful and so powerful in all He could do for others, being marched away like a common thief! Peter could not understand it.

Jesus had known that the bold, impulsive Peter would be afraid. At the Last Supper He had told him something that the disciple had not believed.

"Although you say you would follow me and go with me to imprisonment or death, Peter, I tell you

that before the cock crows twice, you will three
times deny that you know me," He had said to
Peter.

Now Peter, trembling and amazed, was full of
fear as he followed the little company to the house

of Caiaphas, the High Priest. He managed to get into the big courtyard of the house, and he went to a fire to warm himself, for he was cold and miserable.

A maid-servant was there, and she knew him. "You are one of that man's disciples, aren't you?" she said.

"Woman, I have never known Jesus," said Peter, loudly.

Somewhere a cock crowed, for it was almost day.

Then someone else called out to Peter, "You are one of the followers of Jesus."

"Man, I am not," said Peter at once.

And yet a third man said, "Surely this man is one of Jesus' friends—hear how he speaks! He comes from Galilee, like Jesus!"

"I tell you I do not know this man!" shouted Peter, angrily.

Then the cock crowed for the second time, and Peter suddenly remembered what Jesus had said. He had said that Peter would deny Him three times before the cock crowed twice. And in spite of all the brave things he had said to his beloved Master, Peter had been a coward, and had denied that he knew Him.

Poor Peter! With a breaking heart he went out of the courtyard into the street, and wept bitterly.

·THE·END·